WORKING WITH
ASBESTOS
CEMENT

HSG189/2

HSE BOOKS

This guidance is issued by the Health and
Safety Executive. Following the guidance is
not compulsory and you are free to take
other action. But if you do follow the
guidance you will normally be doing
enough to comply with the law. Health and
safety inspectors seek to secure
compliance with the law and may refer to
this guidance as illustrating good practice.

CONTENTS

INTRODUCTION

1   This guidance revises and replaces the HSE guidance note EH71 *Working with asbestos cement and asbestos insulating board* (1996). It describes the properties of asbestos cement (often referred to as AC), and where the material can be found. The guidance gives practical advice on the necessary precautions to prevent exposure to asbestos fibres, or where this is not reasonably practicable, to reduce exposure to asbestos fibres. There are also examples of possible levels of exposure for typical work activities.

2   The guidance does not apply to work with asbestos insulation, asbestos coating, and asbestos insulating board (AIB), which must normally be carried out by specialist contractors licensed by HSE. The Approved Code of Practice *Work with asbestos insulation, asbestos coating and asbestos insulating board* and the HSE publication HSG189/1 *Controlled asbestos stripping techniques for work requiring a licence* provide guidance on working with these materials.

3   The guidance is aimed at anyone who is liable to control or carry out work with asbestos cement including employers, contract managers, site agents, self-employed builders and contractors involved in construction, maintenance, refurbishment and demolition work.

4   Other guidance published by HSE deals with the most immediate risks from asbestos cement: the physical risks of workers falling from or through fragile asbestos cement sheets during construction, maintenance, refurbishment or demolition. Most asbestos cement sheets will not support a person's weight. Falls from, and through, fragile roofs are a major source of deaths in construction work, and precautions to prevent such accidents should receive priority. Advice is contained in the HSE guidance booklet HSG33 *Safety in roof work* (1998).

WHY IS ASBESTOS DANGEROUS?

5   Breathing in asbestos fibres can lead to asbestos-related lung diseases, mainly cancers, which kill more people than any other single work-related illness. The diseases can take from 15 to 60 years to develop - so you and your employees will not be immediately aware of a change in someone's health after breathing in asbestos.

6   There are three main types of asbestos which have been commonly used:

- crocidolite ('blue');
- amosite ('brown');
- chrysotile ('white').

7   All are dangerous, but crocidolite and amosite asbestos are known to be more hazardous than chrysotile. However, the different types cannot usually be identified by their colour alone. Where asbestos is affected by heat and chemicals, or combined with other substances, the colour and appearance can change.

WHAT IS ASBESTOS CEMENT

8   Asbestos cement is predominantly a mixture of cement and asbestos which when in a dry state has a density greater than 1 tonne per cubic metre (1000 kg/m^3). It is a light grey and hard material which generally contains 10% to 15% asbestos fibre, but occasionally can contain up to 40%, bound in a matrix of Portland cement or autoclaved calcium silicate. Asbestos cement differs from AIB in that it is denser and more brittle. A sample of asbestos cement is shown in Figure 1.

9   There are two major groups of asbestos cement products. The first comprises profiled and flat sheets, slates, rainwater goods (gutters, downpipes and troughs), flue pipes and bends, decking tiles, cisterns and sumps. The second group consists solely of asbestos cement pressure pipes for the transport of drinking water, while thinner walled pipes have been used for sewage and drainage.

10   The majority of asbestos cement products contain only chrysotile asbestos but some old products, such as pressure pipes and sheet material, may contain the more hazardous crocidolite or amosite asbestos. Crocidolite asbestos was used between 1950 and 1969, and amosite asbestos from 1945 to around 1980. The importation of crocidolite voluntarily ceased in 1970 and amosite in 1983. The importation, supply and use of crocidolite and amosite was prohibited by the Asbestos (Prohibitions) Regulations 1985.

Figure 1 Example of asbestos cement

11　The use of chrysotile asbestos in fibre cement products increased gradually between 1910 and 1940 and then more rapidly until 1960. Because of the health effects associated with asbestos, increased legislative and public pressure, and technological developments in substitute fibres and non-fibrous alternatives, the use of chrysotile asbestos has declined steadily since the mid 1970s.

12　Some manufacturers have added cellulose pulp to their asbestos cement products. The resulting boards have densities similar to semi-compressed and fully compressed boards. They also exhibit similar strength. This type of asbestos cement was used as flexible partition board and lining, with improved bending strength and lower thermal conductivity. Pigments have been added to these products to give them a different colour, for example light tan, blue, green or red.

13　Asbestos wood is also an asbestos cement mixture, containing approximately 21% asbestos. It was intended for purposes similar to fully compressed flat sheet, where a lighter board was required with good fire protection properties. Asbestos wood has been used on house doors where there was a need for fire protection, and for greater strength than that provided by AIB.

WHAT HAS ASBESTOS CEMENT BEEN USED FOR?

14 Asbestos cement products have been put to wide range of uses, some of which are given in Table 1 (not exhaustive).

Table 1 Asbestos cement products and their uses

Asbestos cement product	Use
Profiled sheets	Roofing, wall cladding and weather boarding.
Semi-compressed flat sheet and partition board	Partitioning in farm buildings and housing, shuttering in industrial buildings, decorative panels for facings, bath panels, soffits, linings to walls and ceilings, portable buildings, propagation beds in horticulture, domestic constructions, fire surrounds, ironing board panels and composite panels for fire protection.
Fully compressed sheet and partition board	As above but where stronger materials are required, for example, laboratory bench topes, external sills, fire surrounds and hearths for electric or gas fires.
Tiles and slates (made from fully compressed flat sheet)	Cladding, decking and promenade tiles. Roofing.
Moulded products	Cisterns and tank, drains, sewer pipes and rain water goods. Flue pipes. Roofing components and accessories (ridges, ventilators, facias, soffits, etc). Cable troughs and conduits. Ventilators and ducts. Window/flower boxes.
Pressure pipes	Water supply, sewage and underground drainage.

15   Asbestos cement products can often be found behind non-asbestos materials or coated with decorative or other coatings, and are therefore not always readily identifiable. They may also be used in areas which are not readily accessible.

16   Asbestos cement products such as roof sheets can often be found in conjunction with other asbestos-containing materials. For example, a warehouse may have an asbestos cement roof which has a sprayed asbestos coating (limpet) on the inner surface. The presence of such materials significantly alters the risk associated with work on the asbestos cement sheets. This is because sprayed coatings are loose friable materials which are easily disturbed, leading to very high exposures. In these circumstances, more stringent precautions are required than for work on asbestos cement alone, and the work needs to be carried out by a specialist contractor holding a licence issued by HSE under the Asbestos (Licensing) Regulations 1983 (as amended). These Regulations apply to any work involving the removal, repair or disturbance of asbestos insulation, asbestos coating and asbestos insulating board. Further information can be found in the HSE publication *A guide to the Asbestos (Licensing) Regulations 1983*.

17   The risks presented by asbestos cement and examples of typical exposures are discussed in Appendix 1.

LEGISLATIVE REQUIREMENTS

The Control of Asbestos at Work Regulations 1987 (as amended) (CAWR)

18   These Regulations apply **to all work with asbestos, including asbestos cement**. Before starting any work where asbestos is present, CAWR requires you to make an assessment of the likely exposure of your employees to asbestos. The assessment needs to be in writing and should cover:

- where it is planned to install an asbestos cement product, the justification for not using a non-asbestos substitute;

- a description of the work; including the type of work and its duration;

- the type, quantity and condition of the asbestos cement;

- the steps taken to prevent or reduce exposure to the lowest level reasonably practicable;

- the reasons for the chosen work methods;

- the steps taken to control the release of asbestos into the environment;

- details of expected exposures and the number of people affected;

- the procedures for the selection, provision, use and decontamination of personal protective equipment (PPE), including respiratory protective equipment (RPE);

■   procedures for the removal of waste;

■   procedures for dealing with emergencies;

■   any other information relevant to safe working.

19 It is not necessary to carry out a full assessment before each individual job if you are carrying out work which involves similar jobs on a number of sites. But where the work varies significantly from site to site, for example in demolition, you will have to carry out a new assessment for each job. A copy of the assessment should be kept readily available on site.

20 The general Approved Code of Practice accompanying CAWR contains more information on carrying out assessments.

21 The Regulations also place a duty on employers to prevent employees being exposed to asbestos by using, where practicable, less hazardous non-asbestos substitutes (see paragraph 30).

Control limits and action levels

22 A control limit is that concentration of asbestos in the air (averaged over any continuous four-hour or ten-minute period) to which employees must not be exposed, unless they are wearing suitable RPE. The four-hour and ten-minute periods have their own control limits, the values of which varies depending on the type of asbestos present. The control limits are given in Table 2.

23 Action levels apply to exposure in the longer term, and are cumulative exposures calculated over any continuous 12-week period. The 12-week period should not be chosen to avoid exceeding an action level; it should represent a 'worst-case' for the work being undertaken. If the exposure of any employee exceeds or is likely to exceed an action level, the regulations in CAWR on notification, designated areas and medical surveillance, apply. The action levels are given in Table 2. The HSE guidance note EH10 *Asbestos: exposure limits and measurement of airborne dust concentrations* contains guidance on how to calculate action levels.

Table 2 Control limits and action levels for asbestos

Asbestos type	4-hr control limit (f/ml)	10-min control limit (f/ml)	Action level (fibrehrs/ml)
Chrysotile alone	0.3	0.9	72
Any other form of asbestos, either alone or in mixtures, including mixtures of chrysotile with any other form of asbestos	0.2	0.6	48

Notes:

f/ml - fibres per millilitre of air averaged over any continuous period.

fibre hours/ml - calculated by multiplying the airborne exposure in f/ml by the time in hours for which it lasts to give exposure in fibre hours/ml. Cumulative exposures calculated by adding together all the individual exposures over the 12-week period in question.

Notification

24   Regulation 6 of CAWR requires you to notify the relevant enforcing authority when you are planning to work with asbestos cement, and when exposure is likely to exceed the action level. The duty to notify only applies on the first occasion when work with asbestos cement is liable to result in exposure exceeding the action level. But where the work varies significantly from job to job, or site to site, you have to notify the enforcing authority each time work is planned (you only need to make a single one-off notification under CAWR if you hold a licence issued under the Asbestos (Licensing) Regulations 1983 (as amended)). More information on notifying work with asbestos cement can be found in the general Approved Code of Practice accompanying CAWR.

25   The enforcing authority will be either HSE or the environmental health department of your local authority, depending on the main activity at the premises where the work is planned. You can check with your local HSE office if you are unsure.

Asbestos (Prohibitions) Regulations 1992

26 The Asbestos (Prohibitions) Regulations 1992 prohibit the import, supply and use of crocidolite and amosite asbestos as well as a number of products containing chrysotile asbestos. The Regulations therefore prohibit the reuse of the older asbestos cement products containing crocidolite or amosite asbestos.

Construction (Design and Management) Regulations 1994 (CDM)

27 These Regulations place duties on clients, clients' agents (where appointed), designers and contractors to ensure that the health and safety aspects of the work are taken into account, and then co-ordinated and managed effectively throughout all the stages of a construction project. This includes all stages in the lifecycle of a project, from conception, design and planning through to the execution of works on site and subsequent construction, maintenance and repair.

28 These Regulations apply to the planning and execution of much construction work which involves asbestos cement. Where CDM applies, the following conditions apply:

- clients should provide information about the location, type and condition of asbestos cement;

- designers should take account of this information by altering their designs to remove or reduce the need to work with asbestos cement;

- planning supervisors should ensure information about asbestos, relevant to the work in hand, is available to designers and the principal contractor;

- the principal contractor should ensure that individual contractors are aware of the relevant information, and workers should be briefed;

■ anyone arranging for someone to undertake construction work should be reasonably satisfied that their appointees are competent to undertake the work safely and without risk to health;

■ where work with asbestos cement is part of the construction work, anyone arranging for someone to do work should be reasonably satisfied that they are competent in work of that type;

■ at the end of a project, a health and safety file should be prepared which includes relevant information about asbestos.

29 Further guidance on the Regulations is given in the Approved Code of Practice *Managing construction for health and safety* which accompanies the CDM Regulations.

SUBSTITUTES FOR ASBESTOS CEMENT

30   There are a number of non-asbestos fibres which can be substituted for asbestos and have been developed for use in fibre cement products. The principal non-asbestos reinforcing fibres currently in use are polyvinylalcohol, aramid and cellulose fibres. These present a lower hazard than chrysotile asbestos and should, where practicable, be used in preference to asbestos to fulfil duties under CAWR. There are also alternative materials which do not rely on fibres, for example, profiled PVC and steel sheeting. Further guidance can be found in the HSE leaflet MISC155 *Substitutes for chrysotile (white) asbestos.*

HOW TO IDENTIFY ASBESTOS CEMENT

31 If you own, manage or have responsibilities for a workplace building which may contain asbestos-containing products (including asbestos cement), you need to think about the risk of exposure to workers and others who may use the building. You need to manage the risk. In order to do this you need to know:

- the location of the asbestos;

- the form of the asbestos (lagging, coating, ceiling tiles, asbestos cement, etc);

- the condition of the asbestos;

- the type of asbestos present.

32 One way of finding this information is to carry out a sampling and analysis survey to identify asbestos-containing materials. Alternatively, you can assume that all suspect materials contain asbestos. In either case, you should note the location of these materials in a register and put a management plan in place to manage the risks. These should be consulted before carrying out any maintenance, refurbishment or demolition work. Further guidance on managing asbestos in buildings is given in the HSE booklet *Managing asbestos in workplace buildings* (INDG223) and *Asbestos materials in buildings* produced by the Department of the Environment (this document is being revised and is due for publication in 1999). Specific guidance on how to manage asbestos cement products already in place is given in Appendix 2.

33 Asbestos surveys should be carried out by people with adequate knowledge, training and experience. Sources of such expertise include the *Directory of occupational hygiene consultants* produced by the British Institute of Occupational Hygienists (01332 298087) (BIOH), Asbestos Testing and Consultancy (01245 269336) (ATAC) who are a division of ARCA (Asbestos Removal Contractors Association), your trade association or the HSE InfoLine (0541 545500). HSE is also preparing guidance on how to carry out building surveys which is due for publication in 1999.

34 A competent laboratory should analyse survey samples. They are likely to be competent if they are accredited by the UK Accreditation Service (UKAS). The HSE publication MDHS77 *Asbestos in bulk materials* and the Department of the Environment publication *Asbestos materials in buildings* contain more information on sampling and analysis of asbestos-containing materials, and on quality assurance and quality control schemes.

35 You may need to determine whether the density of an asbestos-containing board material is less than or greater than 1000 kg/m^3, to classify it as 'board' or 'cement'. The methods adopted for this should be suitable for the material under evaluation, ie they should not give false results by altering the density during the test. Various standard methods are described in BS 4624: 1981, BS 3536 Part 2: 1974, and the guidance on building surveys being prepared by HSE.

HOW TO WORK SAFELY WITH ASBESTOS CEMENT

Planning and preparation

36 An assessment of the proposed work should be carried out, as required by regulation 5 of CAWR (see paragraph 18). The assessment will determine the risk presented by the work and the precautions to take for preventing exposure, or where this is not reasonably practicable, for controlling exposure. It is important to remember that a higher risk is caused by breathing more fibres, either because the concentration is higher or because the exposure is over a longer period.

37 The following general principles should be followed when planning the work (these points are discussed in more detail in subsequent sections):

- where reasonably practicable, avoid working on asbestos cement;

- keep the material wet when working on it;

- where reasonably practicable, avoid using abrasive power and pneumatic tools;

- where reasonably practicable, carry out those higher risk jobs which are absolutely essential at a central point to make supervision, control, cleaning, etc, easier. This includes jobs such as cutting and drilling;

- use cleaning methods which minimise dust disturbance;

- make sure your employees have adequate information on the hazards and risks associated with working with asbestos cement, and are properly trained in the correct working practices and use of control measures.

Area segregation

38   You will need to segregate the work area to prevent the spread of asbestos and the exposure of people not involved in the work. How much you need to do depends on the assessment, for example the risk will be greater within an occupied building compared with work outside. In most cases it is sufficient to mark the work area with signs to prevent non-asbestos workers approaching. But, if the work is likely result in significant disturbance of the asbestos cement, you need to consider erecting a physical barrier. The extent of the barrier will depend on the outcome of the risk assessment carried out before the work starts.

39   A physical barrier should prevent the spread of debris and airborne fibre. This is usually done using the fabric of the building and polythene sheeting. Further guidance on the design and construction of enclosures is provided in the Approved Code of Practice *Work with asbestos insulation, asbestos coating and asbestos insulating board* and the HSE guidance note EH51 *Enclosures provided for work with asbestos insulation, coatings and insulating board.* However, it is unlikely that full enclosure with negative pressure units will be necessary. If your assessment identifies the need for a full enclosure then it might be best to employ a licensed asbestos removal contractor.

40   Whatever means of segregation are used, there is a need to post warning notices. Where a control limit is liable to be exceeded, the notices should say that the area is a 'respirator zone' and RPE must be worn. If the action level is liable to be exceeded, the area should be designated as an 'asbestos area'. Employees not engaged in the work should not be permitted into either of these designated areas.

WORK METHODS

41 Working with asbestos cement products can be divided into two categories:

- installation, repair, maintenance and other similar work;

- removal and demolition.

Installation, repair, maintenance and other similar work

42 Work with asbestos cement can cover a variety of activities such as the installation of asbestos cement products and the repair of existing products, and other small-scale work such as the attachment of fixtures and fittings to asbestos cement sheets. These activities can present different problems and risks. There are a number of general precautions which are common to all work and should be used to prevent or control exposure to asbestos fibres. They can be summarised as follows:

- where practicable, use a non-asbestos material
  (see paragraph 30);

- where reasonably practicable, avoid the need to attach items to asbestos cement or route items such as wiring and pipes through it;

- make sure surfaces that may get covered in dust and debris are covered with polythene sheeting;

- keep the material wet when working on it;

- avoid breaking asbestos cement;

- use hand tools in preference to abrasive power or pneumatic tools;

- where abrasive power or pneumatic tools need to be used, they should be set at the lowest effective speed with additional control measures such as local exhaust ventilation (LEV). Typical measures include:

  - a cowl fitted with LEV located around a drill bit (the cowl should be fitted with a spring so that it remains in contact with the surface of the material as the drill bit penetrates); or

  - shadow vacuuming (this is where the nozzle of a type H (BS 5415) vacuum cleaner, fitted with a suitable attachment, is held as close as possible to the source of fibre release throughout the task);

- wear suitable PPE, including RPE;

- keep the work area clean and tidy;

- avoid the use of cleaning methods such as sweeping which will make dust airborne;

- make sure the work area is thoroughly clean on completion of the work.

43   The weathering of external asbestos cement products can result in the release of small quantities of fibrous debris which can accumulate in areas such as drainage gutters on asbestos cement roofs. This debris can dry out, and subsequent work on such areas can result in exposure. Where reasonably practicable and before any work commences, these areas should be cleaned out, keeping the debris wet. The wet debris can be removed and placed in a suitable container, and disposed of as asbestos waste. Any remaining residues can be removed using a low-dust technique such as damp cloths (disposed of as asbestos waste). Operators may require suitable PPE, including RPE. Great care must be taken as the work may need to take place at a high level, with the associated risk of falls. Further advice is given in the HSE guidance HSG33 *Health and safety in roof work* (1998).

Removal and demolition of asbestos cement sheeting

44 Dismantling and demolishing buildings, roofed or clad with asbestos cement sheet, presents special problems, especially if they are old and crumbling. Many asbestos cement products, such as roof sheets, cladding, drainpipes and gutters, are located at height and therefore present a risk of falls. Asbestos cement sheet is a fragile material, and people must not walk on it. You cannot rely on it to support the weight of a person, even with new sheets. It is important to emphasise that falls from, and through, fragile roofs are a major source of deaths in construction work, and precautions to prevent such accidents should be given priority. Further advice is given in HSE guidance HSG33 *Health and safety in roof work* (1998).

45 In order to minimise exposure and control the spread of asbestos, you need to consider the following general precautions:

- where reasonably practicable, remove the asbestos cement before the rest of the structure is demolished;

- where possible, avoid further breaking the sheets;

- keep the material wet when working on it;

- where possible, lower the material onto a clean hard surface;

- remove waste and debris from the site as soon as possible to prevent it being crushed underfoot or by moving vehicles;

- do not bulldoze broken asbestos cement or sheet into piles;

- do not dry sweep asbestos cement debris;

- dispose of the waste and debris safely.

Manual dismantling methods

46 If asbestos cement sheets are in good condition and it is reasonably practicable to produce a safe system of work and provide safe access, they should be taken down whole. Roof sheets should preferably be removed from underneath with mobile elevating work platforms, for example scissor lifts or cherry pickers.

47 When adopting this method, the sheets should not be dropped or damaged. Methods such as careful transfer to covered lorries or skips, or wrapping intact in polythene sheeting, provide the best form of disposal.

Remote dismantling methods

48 If the sheets are disintegrating or the risk of falls is too great, remote demolition techniques such as deliberate controlled collapse should be used. Remote demolition will give rise to low exposures for the equipment operators, and to those who subsequently load the waste into lorries for disposal.

49 When remote techniques are used, the work area must be continually sprayed with water to suppress the spread of asbestos fibres. The roof sheeting should be broken into the building in a controlled manner onto the floor or hardstanding, for instance by using excavators fitted with suitable demolition attachments. You should ensure that this area is clear of other materials before work commences. The system of work should be designed to minimise breakage of sheets. Before, and while loading the broken sheeting into lorries, you should kept it damp by spraying with water. The lorries should be securely sheeted over to prevent the asbestos waste drying out on its way to the tip.

50 To members of the public, the remote method can appear noisy, dusty and often uncontrolled. They are often concerned about demolition of this type when they know or suspect the building was roofed or clad with asbestos cement. In order to alleviate these concerns about this type of work, contractors can:

■ keep the neighbours informed about the work;

■ carry out background air sampling at the perimeter of the site.

CLEANING WEATHERED ASBESTOS CEMENT

51 After years of use the external surface of asbestos cement may become covered in lichens, algae or moss. For aesthetic reasons or before application of surface coatings, you may need to remove these growths, but only if absolutely necessary as it can result in exposure to asbestos fibres. Operators also must take great care as they may need to carry out the work at high level, with the associated risk of falls. Further advice is given in HSE guidance HSG33 *Health and safety in roof work* (1998). The following techniques have been used:

- dry scraping;

- high-pressure water jetting;

- remote cleaning;

- cleaning with surface biocides.

The following paragraphs describe these techniques in a little more detail.

Dry scraping

52 Dry scraping or wire brushing the asbestos cement results in high exposures to asbestos fibres and should be avoided.

High-pressure water jetting

53 High-pressure water jetting (at 138 bar (2000 psi) and above) is a technique which has been used in the past. But there are several problems with this method:

- the jet causes the cement matrix to disintegrate, releasing unbound asbestos fibres;

- the asbestos fibres have no chance of absorbing the water;

- a vast amount of virtually unmanageable slurry, containing free asbestos fibres, is produced which can readily contaminate surrounding areas;

- the jet can cause serious injury.

54 There have been several examples of untrained personnel carrying out this work, without the proper precautions and supervision. This has resulted in exposure of the operators (and others not involved in the work) to asbestos fibres, and in gross contamination of buildings and surrounding areas. Subsequent clean-up operations have proved very expensive.

55 Because of the problems associated with this technique, it should only be used in exceptional circumstances by specialist contractors with well-trained personnel and under close supervision. If you are considering this technique, you should discuss it first with the enforcing authority (HSE or the environmental health department) with responsibility for that site.

Remote cleaning

56 There are remotely operated units available with enclosed rotary cleaning heads which use high-pressure jets and brushes to clean asbestos cement roof sheets. This system has the advantage of the operator being remote from the immediate cleaning area. But, provision still needs to be made to collect the resulting slurry. The manufacturer's operating instructions should be followed closely and the equipment operated by workers who have received specific training and are properly supervised. Operators must take great care as they may need to carry out the work at high level, with the associated risk of falls. Further advice is given in HSE guidance HSG33 *Health and safety in roof work* (1998).

Cleaning with surface biocides

57 There is a range of approved pesticide products which can be used to kill plant material growing on asbestos cement surfaces. These are listed in the guide to approved pesticides (the Blue Book), published annually by the Stationery Office.

58 Products containing salts of dichlorophen or o-phenylphenol, or benzalkonium chloride (quaternary ammonium salts), will kill plant material. These cause no damage to asbestos cement if they are used at the recommended concentrations during non-frosty conditions. The biocides should be applied as low-pressure sprays or as washes.

59   Once moss and algae are dead, they can be removed with water, using gentle brushing. However, dead lichen crusts and ivy roots are unlikely to be removed so easily and these are probably better left where they are. You should note that the roots of mosses may well hold loosened asbestos fibre.

60   This method is preferable to the use of gentle wet brushing alone for moss and algae because the pesticide product will first loosen their hold on the asbestos cement, making removal easier. However, operators need to take great care as they may need to carry out the work at high level, with the associated risk of falls. Further advice is given in HSE guidance HSG33 *Health and safety in roof work* (1998).

THE BEHAVIOUR OF ASBESTOS CEMENT IN FIRES

61 Asbestos fibres can change their mineral structure following prolonged exposure to heat. But research has shown that in fires, only the outer layers of the asbestos material are altered with the interior often remaining unaffected. This means that there will still be hazardous asbestos fibres present in debris and ash.

62 Exposure to the heat of a fire can also cause the cement content of asbestos cement roofing, cladding, etc, to violently rupture, discharging asbestos fibres into the atmosphere and spreading debris over a wide area. Fire can also weaken the binding material in asbestos cement, resulting in fibres being released more easily if the solid debris or ash from the fire is disturbed. The emergency services, building occupants and contractors involved in remedial work will be those most likely to be exposed following a fire.

63 Before taking any remedial action, you should determine the types of asbestos-containing materials present in the building, for example from an asbestos register. The risk from debris and ash, containing only asbestos cement, will be low as long as a number of simple precautions are taken when decontaminating the area:

- the contaminated area should be cordoned off and warning notices posted;

- only essential personnel should enter the cordoned off area;

- personnel should wear suitable PPE, including RPE;

- disturbance of ash and debris should be kept to a minimum;

- the debris should be carefully dampened down, avoiding over-wetting, and carefully removed, for example by shovelling;

- larger pieces of debris should be picked up by hand and placed in a strong plastic bag.

64   Where other asbestos-containing materials such as asbestos insulation, asbestos coating, or AIB are present in the building, then more stringent precautions will be required and the work carried out by a licensed asbestos removal contractor.

DECONTAMINATION AND CLEANING

65 When working with asbestos cement, employees should clean up at the end of each stage of a job to prevent the accumulation of debris and dust. As a minimum, this should be at the end of each shift, but more frequent cleaning will normally be necessary. They should use low dust cleaning methods. Once the work is complete, all surfaces should be given a final clean, again using low dust methods, before the area is handed back for normal occupation.

66 The following cleaning methods can be used:

- Where possible, very large pieces or whole sheets of asbestos cement should not be broken or cut for disposal as this can result in the release of asbestos fibres. They are best disposed of by careful transfer to covered lorries or skips, or by wrapping in polythene sheeting or other suitable material before disposal.

- Small pieces of asbestos cement debris and dust deposits should preferably be removed using a Type H vacuum cleaner (BS 5415). Where they are too big for vacuuming or where there is a significant amount of debris spread over a wide area, it may be more practical to collect the debris and place it in a suitable container. This should be double wrapped, to prevent the escape of fibres, and labelled to show that they contain asbestos (see paragraph 72).

67 The external surfaces of waste containers should be cleaned before removal from the work area.

68 Once the work is complete, a supervisor or foreman should carry out a final inspection to confirm that all the asbestos debris has been removed and the work area adequately cleaned.

69 Workers involved in clearing up asbestos debris need to wear suitable PPE, including RPE (see paragraphs 78 to 85).

WASTE DISPOSAL

70 Asbestos waste, defined as containing more than 0.1% w/w asbestos in the waste, is subject to the waste management controls set out in the Special Waste Regulations 1996. These Regulations require the waste to be consigned to a site which is authorised to accept asbestos waste. This is enforced by the Environment Agency or local authorities in England and Wales, and the Scottish Environment Protection Agency in Scotland.

71 Whatever type of waste container (for example, plastic sacks) is used, it is important to emphasise that the container should be:

- made of a material which in normal handling is strong enough to contain the waste and which takes account, if necessary, of materials in the waste sharp enough to cause punctures;

- capable of being readily decontaminated before leaving the work area;

- kept secure on site until sent for disposal for example in a locked skip;

- properly labelled (see Appendix 3).

72 In certain circumstances, the following regulations may apply to the waste material:

- the Carriage of Dangerous Goods (Classification, Packaging and Labelling) and the Transportable Pressure Receptacles Regulations 1996;

- the Carriage of Dangerous Goods by Road Regulations 1996;

- the Carriage of Dangerous Goods by Rail Regulations 1996.

Where these regulations do not apply, Schedule 2 of CAWR applies.

Further guidance can be found in:

- *The carriage of dangerous goods explained. Part 1: guidance for consignors of dangerous goods by road and rail (classification, packaging and provision of information)* HSG160;

- *The carriage of dangerous goods explained. Part 2: guidance for road vehicle operators and others involved in the carriage of dangerous goods by road* HSG161.

AIR MONITORING

73 The need for air monitoring should be determined as part of the assessment of the work. It may be required for one or more of the following reasons:

- to confirm airborne concentrations of asbestos fibres are as low as reasonably practicable and that the correct choice of RPE has been made;

- to confirm that there has been no measurable spread of airborne fibres to areas adjacent to where work with asbestos cement has taken place;

- to confirm that the work area has been adequately cleaned before being returned to normal use.

74 Air monitoring is not always required but may be of particular importance where:

- large quantities of asbestos cement have been handled;

- the work involved using abrasive power or pneumatic tools and/or breakage of the material; or

- where significant contamination occurred.

75 As an employer, you must only engage laboratories to carry out air monitoring who can demonstrate that they conform to European Standard EN 45001 by accreditation with a recognised accreditation body. You can obtain a list of accredited laboratories from UKAS (0181 917 8400), the *Directory of occupational hygiene consultants* produced by BIOH (01332 298087), Asbestos Testing and Consultancy (01245 269336) (ATAC) who are a division of ARCA (Asbestos Removal Contractors Association), or your trade association. Information is also available from the HSE InfoLine (0541 545500).

76 If you wish to carry out your own air monitoring, you should make sure that employees carrying out the monitoring receive similar standards of training, supervision and quality control to those required by EN 45001.

77 Further guidance on air monitoring is given in the HSE guidance notes EH10 *Asbestos: exposure limits and measurement of airborne dust concentrations* and MDHS39/4 *Asbestos fibres in air.*

RPE FOR WORK WITH ASBESTOS CEMENT

78 RPE should not be used as the only means of controlling exposure. Before considering the use of RPE, airborne asbestos fibre concentrations should be reduced as low as is reasonably practicable by other means. If despite these precautions, the exposure of your employees to asbestos fibres is likely to exceed the control limit then you must always provide suitable RPE. This should reduce exposure as low as reasonably practicable and in any case below the control limit.

79 Always remember to choose RPE which protects employees to a level of exposure well within the upper limit of its protection range. If in doubt, always select higher performance equipment, providing that it is suitable.

80 The HSE booklet INDG264 *Selecting suitable respiratory protective equipment for work with asbestos* can help in the selection of suitable RPE.

81 **Remember, you should never rely on RPE as your main method of controlling exposure. RPE is no substitute for good fibre suppression.**

PROTECTIVE CLOTHING FOR WORK WITH ASBESTOS CEMENT

82 The type of protective clothing provided will depend on the likely exposure and should be suitable for the job. As a general rule, employees need to be provided with protective clothing if a significant amount of asbestos dust is liable to get on their clothes. You should regard any deposit of dust which can be seen as significant.

83 Disposable overalls are normally preferable to cotton type overalls as this removes the need for sending them to a laundry suitably equipped to handle clothing contaminated with asbestos. However, the final choice will depend on the assessment and the suitability of the protective clothing for the work, for example working outside in cold and wet conditions may require waterproof clothing.

84 Contaminated clothing should be vacuumed using a Type H vacuum cleaner (BS 5415), and removed on leaving the work area for breaks and at the end of the work period. It should be stored separately from clean clothing. It must **never** be taken home for cleaning. Arrangements need to be made with a specialised laundry equipped to deal with asbestos-contaminated clothing, and you must follow their procedures for packaging the laundry. Waterproof clothing needs to be sponged or wiped clean.

85 Disposable overalls should be disposed of as asbestos waste at the end of each shift.

CLEANING AND HYGIENE FACILITIES

86   Facilities need to be provided for employees to wash thoroughly after working with asbestos cement. The type and extent of the washing facilities depend on the nature and degree of exposure to asbestos. Where exposure is low and infrequent, for example with minor repair work, the facilities may be shared with other employees who are not likely to be exposed to asbestos.

87   However, you normally need separate hygiene facilities where it is likely that protective clothing may become significantly contaminated with asbestos, for example where:

- large quantities of asbestos cement have been handled;

- the work involves using abrasive power or pneumatic tools and/or breakage of the material;

- significant contamination needs to be removed.

Where this level of contamination is likely to occur, you should consider employing a licensed asbestos removal contractor.

88   More information on the provision and use of hygiene facilities can be found in the HSE guidance note EH47 *The provision, use and maintenance of hygiene facilities for work with asbestos insulation and coatings.*

APPENDIX 1: THE RISK POSED BY ASBESTOS CEMENT PRODUCTS

1   Because the fibres in asbestos cement products are firmly bound in the material, they will only be released if the product is subject to mechanical damage (for example the use of abrasive tools, breakage, etc) or as a result of weathering (coated asbestos cement can be resistant to light abrasion and impact). This contrasts with other asbestos-containing materials such as sprayed coatings and lagging which generally have a greater fibre content and, being loosely bound, release fibres relatively easily when damaged or disturbed. The level of risk therefore depends on the ease by which fibres are released and the type of asbestos present.

2   Asbestos cement products such as roof sheets which are used externally will weather slowly. The low rate of fibre release means that the risk of exposure is extremely low if the sheets are left undisturbed. But the reuse of asbestos cement products, for example in agricultural buildings, is likely to release higher fibre concentrations than the use of new sheets.

3   After several years of external use, asbestos cement may become covered in lichen, algae or moss. Although such growths should rarely have a noticeable effect on the strength, durability or lifetime of asbestos cement, they may become visually unattractive (in some areas they can actually be regarded as mellow and pleasing, and therefore encouraged). If these growths are removed without taking adequate precautions, it can result in fibre release and high exposures (see paragraphs 51 to 60).

4   Table 3 gives examples of typical exposures during work with asbestos cement.

Table 3 Typical fibre concentrations for work with asbestos cement

Activity		Typical exposure (f/ml)
Machine sawing with exhaust ventilation		Up to 2
Machine cutting without exhaust ventilation		
- abrasive disc cutting		15 - 25
- circular saw		10 - 20
- jig saw		2 - 10
Hand sawing		up to 1
Machine drilling		up to 1
Removal of asbestos cement sheeting		up to 0.5
Stacking of asbestos cement sheets		up to 0.5
Remote demolition of asbestos cement structures dry*		up to 0.1
Remote demolition of asbestos cement structures wet*		up to 0.01
Cleaning asbestos cement	Roofing	Vertical cladding
Dry brushing (wire)	3	5 - 8
Wet brushing (wire)	1 - 3	1 - 2

* Subsequent sweeping up after remote demolition may give rise to concentrations greater than 1 f/ml.

1   Inclusion of a technique does not indicate that it is acceptable (eg machine cutting without exhaust ventilation). These concentrations are given to illustrate the high exposures which can result if good work practices are not followed.

2   The exposures quoted are based on measurements taken by HSE. The same process in different locations may result in higher or lower concentrations.

3   The exposures relate to the work period and are not calculated as time-weighted averages.

4   Selection of a figure from the tables is not in itself an assessment. Consideration should be given to whether it is reasonably practicable to use methods which give lower values.

5   HSE is in the process of updating these figures.

APPENDIX 2: HOW TO MANAGE ASBESTOS CEMENT ALREADY IN PLACE

1   Once an asbestos survey has been carried out, you should know, as far as reasonably practicable, the location and condition of the asbestos cement. Some may be damaged or liable to be damaged as a result of its location, some may be in good condition, and some in areas due for maintenance, refurbishment or demolition. Based on this information, you need to make a decision on what remedial action is required and on how to manage the asbestos cement.

2   There is a difference in the risk presented by asbestos cement located inside or outside a building. Inside the building, the asbestos cement may be at greater risk of accidental damage or disturbance, and any fibres released may be close to the occupants, or accumulate and be disturbed later. This needs to be taken into account when making a decision on how to deal with the material.

3   **For asbestos materials including asbestos cement, which are in good condition and are not likely to be disturbed, you can leave them where they are and manage them.**

4   If the asbestos cement is only slightly damaged, it can be repaired and sealed, the material left where it is and managed. Where there is external asbestos cement cladding on a building, you normally only need to seal the internal surfaces, as it is damage or abrasion to these areas that can cause the release of fibres. It is not normally necessary to seal internal surfaces at high level, because the location of the material means that disturbance is unlikely. But ultimately the assessment of the material by the surveyor will determine whether any surface needs to be sealed.

5   Sealing involves the application of a coating (polymeric, bituminous or cement based paint), the type of which will depend on the nature of the material, the level of damage and protection.

6   The coating should adhere firmly to the surface of the asbestos cement. Where the surface of the asbestos cement is dusty and may not permit a good coating, it can be prepared by cleaning with a Type H

(BS 5415) vacuum cleaner or wiped with a damp cloth (which should be disposed of as asbestos waste). You can use an alkaline resistant primer or other suitable material (asbestos cement is alkaline) to prime the surfaces for sealing, before applying the top coat.

7   Where it is possible that some damage may reoccur, instead of removing the asbestos cement it can be enclosed. This involves repairing any minor damage and then covering the asbestos cement with a non-asbestos material, forming a physical barrier. However, resistance to the spread of fire must be maintained. The enclosed area between the covering and the asbestos cement should be sealed, and adequate cavity fire barriers constructed.

8   You need to consider removing asbestos cement if it is in a poor condition, or is likely to be damaged or disturbed as a result of building maintenance, refurbishment or demolition works, or the normal activities (or a planned change of use for a location) within an area.

9   Further guidance on managing asbestos in buildings is given in the HSE booklet INDG223 *Managing asbestos in workplace buildings* and *Asbestos materials in buildings* produced by the Department of the Environment (this document is being revised and is due for publication in 1999).

APPENDIX 3: LABELLING REQUIREMENTS FOR PLASTIC BAGS/SACKS CONTAINING ASBESTOS WASTE

Waste blue asbestos (crocidolite)	UN 2212	Carriage of Dangerous Goods (Classification, Packaging and Labelling) and Use of Transportable Pressure Receptacles Regulations 1996
Waste brown asbestos (amosite)	UN 2212	
Waste white asbestos (chrysotile)	UN 2590	

Regulations 7 and 8 refer

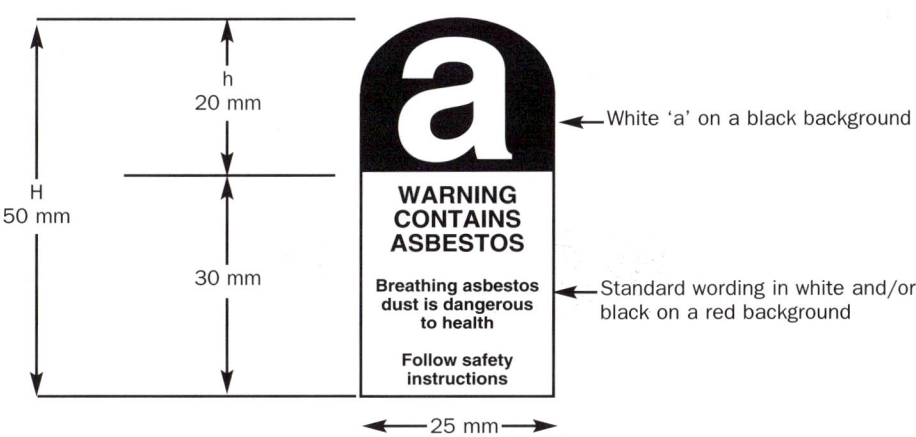

h 20 mm

H 50 mm

30 mm

WARNING CONTAINS ASBESTOS

Breathing asbestos dust is dangerous to health

Follow safety instructions

White 'a' on a black background

Standard wording in white and/or black on a red background

25 mm

The dimensions in millilitres of the label shall be those shown on the diagram, except that larger measurements may be used, but in that case the dimension of the label indicated as h, on the diagram above, shall be 40% of the dimension indicated as H on that diagram.

The label shall be clearly and indelibly printed so that the words in the lower half of the label can be easily read, and those words shall be printed in black or white.

REFERENCES

1   *The Asbestos (Licensing) Regulations 1983* SI 1983/1649 HMSO 1983 ISBN 0 11 037649 8 as amended by the *Asbestos (Licensing) (Amendment) Regulations 1998* SI 1998/3233 Stationery Office 1998 ISBN 0 11 080279 9

2   *Controlled asbestos stripping techniques for work requiring a licence* HSG189/1 HSE Books 1999 ISBN 0 7176 1666 5

3   *Selecting respiratory protective equipment for work with asbestos* INDG264 HSE Books 1997 (revised edition due in Spring 1999)

4   *Health and safety in roof work* HSG33 HSE Books 1998 ISBN 0 7176 1425 5

5   *The Control of Asbestos at Work Regulations* 1987 SI 1987/2115 HMSO 1987 ISBN 0 11 078115 5 as amended by the *Control of Asbestos at Work (Amendment) Regulations 1992* SI 1992/3068 HMSO 1992 ISBN 0 11 025738 3 and the *Control of Asbestos at Work (Amendment) Regulations 1998* SI 1998/3235 Stationery Office 1998 ISBN 0 11 080277 2

6   *The control of asbestos at work. Control of Asbestos at Work Regulations 1987. Approved Code of Practice* Third edition L27 HSE Books 1999 ISBN 0 7176 1674 6

7   *Work with asbestos insulation, asbestos coating and asbestos insulating board. Control of Asbestos at Work Regulations 1987. Approved Code of Practice* Third edition L28 HSE Books 1999 ISBN 0 7176 1674 6

8   *Asbestos (Prohibitions) Regulations 1992* SI 1992/3067 HMSO 1992 ISBN 0 11 025740 5

9   *Construction (Design and Management) Regulations 1994* SI 1994/3140 HMSO 1994 ISBN 0 11 043845 0 (CDM Regulations)

10 *Managing construction for health and safety. The Construction (Design and Management) Regulations 1994. Approved Code of Practice* L54 HSE Books 1995 ISBN 0 7176 0792 5

11 *Enclosures provided for work with asbestos insulation, coatings and insulation board* EH51 HSE Books 1989 ISBN 0 11 885408 9

12 *Pesticides 1998: pesticides approved under the Control of Pesticides Regulations 1986 and the Plant Protection Products Regulations 1995* Stationery Office 1998 ISBN 0 11 243032 5 (the Blue Book)

13 *The carriage of dangerous goods explained. Part 1: guidance for consignors of dangerous goods by road and rail (classification, packaging, labelling and provision of information)* HSG160 HSE Books 1996 ISBN 0 7176 1255 4

14 *The carriage of dangerous goods explained. Part 2: guidance for road vehicle operators and others involved in the carriage of dangerous goods* HSG161 HSE Books 1996 ISBN 0 7176 1253 8

15 *Special Waste Regulations 1996* SI 1996/972 HMSO 1996 ISBN 0 11 062941 8

16 *Asbestos: exposure limits and measurement of airborne dust concentrations* EH10 HSE Books 1995 ISBN 0 7176 0907 3

17 *Asbestos fibres in air: sampling and evaluation by phase contrast microscopy (PCM) under the Control of Asbestos at Work Regulations* MDHS39/4 HSE Books 1995 ISBN 0 7176 1113 2

18 *Substitutes for chrysotile (white) asbestos* MISC155 HSE Books 1998

19 Department of the Environment *Asbestos material in buildings* HMSO 1991 ISBN 0 11 752370 4

While every effort has been made to ensure the accuracy of the references listed in this publication, their future availability cannot be guaranteed.

Printed and published by the Health and Safety Executive   C80 02/99